Table of Contents

Yoga For Fast Weight Loss, Amazing Energy, Fighting Stress, Increasing Motivation and a New You!

Transformative Tranquility: Meditation Fast Start Guide To Lose Weight, Create Amazing Abundance and Live Stress Free Effortlessly

Yoga For Fast Weight Loss, *Amazing Energy,*

Fighting Stress, Increasing Motivation and a New You!

Daniel Amos

Introduction

Watch your body, mind and spirit all be raised as *"Yoga For Weight Loss, instantly and incredibly* Increases Your Energy, Getting You Ready For a **Transformative** New *You*. Using strategies for beginning yoga, you will fast become a yogini (female yoga practitioner) or yogi (male practitioner) orchestrating an immensely gratifying mind, body and soul connection.

Following these stress and anxiety *de-stressors* you will find it easy to implement the strategies laid forth in this text to start melting the pounds 15quickly and easily. Not only that you'll keep those pesky pounds away without stress.

This fast start guide is not only a fantastic tool for weight loss and amazing vibrant energy, diminishing stress and anxiety, but you will use it as a lifestyle changing tool.

If you're finding that you struggle with weight loss, low energy and motivation, or stress, *now* might be the time to look into the wonderful benefits of yoga to start transforming into the new you today!

Not only are their fantastic ways to lose weight, decrease stress and live a fantastically re-energized life described in exciting detail contained within the pages of this book, but as an added bonus you will be receiving an amazing collection of *70 hatha yoga poses with full, professional video instruction* to further you along the path to weight loss and extreme health.

Also, if you act now you will receive a fantastic bonus and, available only for a short time…

4 incredible meditation audios *(each one is 4 parts)*, with full featured accompanying script pdfs which include: Accelerated healing meditation, reach your potential meditation, higher power meditation, quiet the mind meditation, and serenity mediations. All amazing *free bonuses just for giving this everything-yoga-book-on-weight-loss a try*.

All you have to do is sign up for our free newsletter link found at the end of this e-book.

So if you haven't done so, make sure to download right now and start enjoying, not only this amazing book but all of the incredible bonuses right now.

Raise your vibration, raise your life!
Daniel Amos

Preface: A Warm-up to Yoga or I AM Bowing to You Now

You've probably heard of yoga at some point in your life, especially considering how widespread the practice has become in many cultures today. So what is it? Is it an exercise? Is it a type of meditation? A food you can buy in the dairy aisle of the supermarket?

Actually, it's a combination of the first two: *a mix of exercise and meditation.*

Yoga is rooted into Buddhist and Indian culture. It consists of putting your body in certain positions or poses (asanas) while using breath control, with the ultimate goal of being relaxed. It is an exercise that improves health and calms stress, as yoga is used for its many mental, emotional, and physical benefits. Part of the concept of this exercise is that it helps not only to calm the body, but with focus being on controlling your breathing and holding positions that work to stretch and relax muscles, it also calms the mind. It takes the focus away from every-day stresses and worries and brings it toward your body. Having that kind of control over yourself aids in helping you feel strong, confident, in control, and less stressed.

Now, these are just the basics! Though this is a simple overview of how yoga works and what it can do for you, the possibilities are endless. People have used yoga to relieve symptoms of serious illnesses, to lose weight, to help with mental stresses, and to cure common ailments. In other words, yoga can turn your life around and help you on your path toward change!

So grab your yoga mat and your exercise/comfortable clothes, because you'll want to get started right away. This is a detailed overview of just what yoga can do for you. We will be exploring some fantastic possibilities and show you how to use yoga to lose weight, keep more energy, and to further transforming yourself into a newer, better you!

Yoga – Start Reaping the Benefits Today!

Yoga is a type of exercise where you keep your body in specific poses while breathing evenly in order to stay focused, stay calmer, and strengthen your body. Poses such as the sun salutation and downward dog require you to stretch, move, or hold your body in one pose for up to a minute while keeping steady breathing. This requires concentration, calm, and mental strength, as well as muscle control. While you are keeping your body still and focusing on doing just that, your body and mind learn a level of self-discipline that opens the doors for improved functioning. When you feel more in control, you can be limitless!

Benefits for your Mind

The concentration that yoga requires makes for a stronger mind. Once you can harness all your energy and keep the focus on your breathing and the still position in which you must hold your body, you gain strength of the mind, and with that strength you will find yourself performing better on a day-to-day basis. Studies have shown that disciplining the brain to coordinate with the body for exercises such as yoga and athletic sports can increase brain function to increase memory, improve emotional self-regulation, fight depression, manage stress, and lift mood. In other words, you may be feeling better about your life simply because your mind is becoming better at handling life's curveballs and seeing through tough times. These are just some of the benefits yoga is able to bring to the mind!

Stress Reliever

This will be briefly touched upon again in chapter 3 (as it is also one of the main reasons yoga is so effective for weight loss), that yoga is able to lower the produced stress hormones and lower the existing level of hormones in the body. Feeling stressed releases cortisol into the body, and one of the biggest downsides of having excess cortisol is it's function of storing fat. When we are stresses, we often shut down body signals like needing to eat or sleep in order to perform the task we have at hand. This makes the body believe it is in a "state of emergency," and therefore must hold onto its resources for energy because it does not know when it will get replenished next. Because of this, cortisol holds on to fat. Reducing stress means reducing cortisol levels, and makes your body relax as it can get out of panic mode!

Yoga is Good For the Body, Too!

As you'll see when you read along, yoga can help you lose weight as well as affect the hormones produced in the body that can wear down your health. When you exercise or relax with yoga, you are moving your body by expending energy through your muscle motions and breathing. Any type of action is burning calories and using up the energy resources in the body, and yoga is no different! Make it part of your exercise routine and yoga will improve the health of not just your mind, but your body, too.

In addition to this, yoga will boost your energy, like exercising does. The benefits from doing yoga or making it a habit are seen across the board. Do you think you're ready to take on yoga and see what it has in store for you? You can get started right now!

Let's take a look at how you can get started with some tricks and techniques that will keep you on the path to transforming your body and mind, even in small ways! Make sure you have a bottle of water, comfortable and flexible clothing, and a yoga mat (can be bought at most retail sports stores) so you can protect your feet and joints from the hardness of the floor.

Yoga Tricks and Techniques That Will Keep You Motivated to Transform Your Life!

So how to begin your new endeavor in search of the pros of doing yoga? In this chapter, we will give you a few posing techniques that should start you off in the right direction. You may keep this chapter as a reference or refresher once you get into the swing of things. There are also many store-bought books that can help you advance your yoga skills and give you new insights if you'd like to take it further. Remember, trial-and-error is the best way to choose poses that will help you personally.

If something is a little too hard or strenuous, do not pursue it. This may end up doing more harm than good to your body, and in addition, will make you less excited about doing yoga. If an exercise is too easy, step it up a little bit. We will be able to share some ways you can do this with the following suggestions.

As for our Yoga Tricks and Techniques, let's take a look at the positions that are the most helpful in losing weight and retaining energy, so you can get a jump-start toward your goals!

Position 1: The Half Moon

This pose tones the buttocks and thighs. Stand with feet on the ground, together and touching. Raise your hands above your head and grasp at the palms, reaching high as if trying to touch the ceiling. Inhale. Exhale, and slowly bend your whole body sideways from your hips, as if to resemble the crescent curve of the moon, all while keeping your hands together. Avoid bending forward as this disrupts the muscle stretch, and do your best to keep your elbows straight. You should feel the pull of a stretch from your clasped hands in a line down to your thighs while you complete this pose.

Now you can inhale, and bring your body back to the original position. When you repeat this pose, repeat it on the other side. Hold this pose for 3-5 breaths.

Click For Video Demonstration => 29 Half Moon Left

Click For Video Demonstration => 30 Half Moon Right

Position 2: Hover/Plank

This position is traditionally known in exercise as a floor plank, so the name should hopefully stir up a familiar image in your mind. If not, this pose will mean letting your body "hover" in a position that is straight and parallel to the floor. To begin, get into the push-up position with hands flat on the floor, legs and torso extended straight back, propped up on your tiptoes. Make sure your hands are directly underneath your shoulders. Start by exhaling and lowering yourself toward the floor, while bending the elbows back and keeping your arms close to your body. Keep your abdomen tight and hold the position at a couple of inches above the floor. Repeat for around three to five breaths.

To make this a little easier, feel free to keep knees on the floor as you do this pose. To add a tougher element, do a reverse leg lift by extended a leg a few inches into the air while you are in the "hold" position. Repeat with the other leg.

Click For Video Demonstration => Beginner High Plank

Position 3: The Chair

This is another great fat-burning position that will help you lose weight and tone the buttocks and thighs. You can begin this pose much like the others, standing straight while keeping feet close together on the floor. Keep your toes facing ahead of you and your arms relaxed at the sides. When you inhale, raise your arms above you with your palms facing each other, as if trying to contain something between your hands. At the exhale, sit back at about a 45-degree angle while keeping your knees behind your toes, and your abs tightened to strengthen your core and support your back.

This is also traditionally known as a "squat." Want to lessen the sting? Keep your feet hip-distance apart with your hand on your thighs rather than straight with hands at the sides, and when you sit back, make it only at a 30-degree angle. For an added challenge, using the originally outlined pose, lift your hells off the floor when you move to sit back, while balancing on the balls of your feet.

Click For Video Demonstration => 21 Chair Pose Side

Position 4: Rocking Boat

This one may be trickier for beginners, but it is possible and satisfying to complete! This pose will target your abdomen and your back muscles. Sit on your yoga mat with your knees bent and feet positioned flat on the floor. Place your hands on your thighs. With your torso straight and your head aligned with your body, stretch back in a lean of about 45 degrees, raising your feet so that your calves are positioned parallel to floor, keeping the toes pointed. When you begin to inhale, you extend both your arms and legs. Make sure your legs stay together! Now you can exhale. At the following inhale lower your torso and legs a little further so that your body forms a wide "V." Exhale, and while you do, raise your torso and legs. You can try extending your arms in this position for more muscle resistance and a greater challenge. Repeat this for three to five breaths. If you're having a little bit of difficulty, try holding the back of your thighs with your hands and keep your legs bent instead of extending them, so you only have to lower your torso. Click here for rock the boat video demonstration

Position 5: The Willow Tree

This pose is great for keeping firmer the sides of your abdomen, and is also one of the best for weight loss. Here's how to get into it: Stand with your feet on the floor, together, while you let your arms fall at your sides. Place the bottom of your left foot on the inside of your right thigh, with your knee bending outward to the side. This may be difficult at first as it requires a bit of skill in balance, but don't put too much pressure on yourself; Go slowly until you can hold the pose, and remember to breathe while staying patient. If it proves difficult, make it easier by lowering the placement of your foot or keeping them flat on the floor. Now, touch your palms in front of your chest for two breaths. As you near the end of your second breath, extend your arms upward, with your fingers pointing toward the ceiling. Exhale, finally, and when you inhale again, for your third breath, bend your entire torso to the left. As you inhale once more, move to straighten your body to its original posture. Alternate between which feet you use to place on the inside of your thigh. Three to five breathes to hold this should do the trick. Want to kick it up a notch? Try this pose while closing your eyes!

These are five of the basic fat-burning poses that will be most helpful toward your goal of losing weight. There are many, many yoga poses that can be tapped into that are used to strengthen your core, tackle stress areas, or simply to release muscle tension. Don't be shy about looking for different yoga poses that will help in the way you need it most!

Click For Video Demonstration => <u>44 Three Legged Dog Left</u>

Click For Video Demonstration => <u>47 Tree Pose Right Side</u>

Amazing Ways Yoga Can Help You Lose Those Stubborn Pounds!

Yoga is like exercise, and uses breathing and motion as an aerobic exercise that will keep you healthy and active for years to come. Using proper breathing techniques can help bring more oxygen to the blood and to the brain, eventually helping control your "life energy," the resource you pull from to expend energy. This is a spiritual concept, of course, that was laid out dating back to traditional yoga practices. However, this can absolutely hold true when talking about your body's natural response to your movements and breathing as well. After all, our "energy" comes from the food we eat, and an excess of that or even insufficient burning of a normal amount of caloric intake can keep more weight on us than we'd like!

Burning Off the Pounds

Since yoga has been shown to reduce stress while making the body and mind calmer, this will inevitably have an effect on the body, too. A deeper look into your body's physical reaction to yoga shows that this activity lowers your stress hormone levels, while encouraging insulin sensitivity. What does this mean?

It means that while doing yoga, your body is being signaled to burn the food you've eaten for fuel, rather than storing those calories you just ate as fat. One of the best benefits of stress-lowering is that your body can function at its highest form instead of being held back by emotional and mental weight. Therefore, this technique is not only a great way to lose weight, but it's a fantastic preventative for gaining weight as well!

Daily Routine

Make yoga an integral part of your life. Keeping to a schedule of when you will make time for yoga will help you stay motivated, prevent you from making excuses about "not having time" if you schedule in advance, and will make for a steady improvement in your weight. Remember to use varying yoga techniques each day, and to make sure your routine is not so strict that you are doing the same exercises and poses every day. You can reference the earlier mentioned five poses and do a combination of three of them each day, or look to your own books and searches for new poses that you'd like to alternate between. Anything you want to do to switch it up will help keep your body guessing, instead of creating a resistance to your routines!

When and How Often?

If you want to lose weight with yoga, the key is to keep it to a manageable level. What many people don't realize is that excessive workouts on a daily basis, though technically burning calories, are an ineffective way to lose weight. Working out without rest periods mean muscle mass is growing rapidly and the body is too preoccupied creating new muscle tissue to gather stored energy away from your fat. In other words, even when engaging in something as low-maintenance as yoga, you need to give yourself some rest periods.

If you're going to hold your yoga poses for 3 – 5 breaths, and you want to try and make time for it every day, you'll be on the right track. However, holding your poses for longer than 5 breaths (going up to 8 and beyond) will put just a little extra strain on your muscles, and may require a day off to rest. The typical medical standard for muscle rest in order to continue a fat-burning cycle is 48 hours. This is why most professionals and institutes suggest working out three times a week – that gives you the minimum of 48 hours to rest your muscles and have time to recover to get back to it!

Try doing no more than 3 or 4 poses for 3 – 5 breaths each day, and with any more than that, switch your routine to doing it 3 times a week. This will ensure you're getting the best weight-loss results, and will force the stubborn pounds that are lingering behind to finally let go!

How To Feel Rejuvenated From All That Extra Energy

When you do anything that expends energy, or anything that is an exception to sitting or standing motionless, you get your body's systems in motion. This puts your body on a path to "keep going," as the energy is you're using is going into a natural body cycle that is creating more energy. Rather, it is *releasing* the energy you have stored. When you do yoga, you'll find that you have a spurt of energy and over time, you'll begin accumulating extra energy and motivation to do more of the things you want! Here's how to harness that extra energy you'll be feeling to get rejuvenated rather than sitting still and allowing it to get stored back into your body, unused.

You Are What You Eat

Eating will be the best way to supplement your energy gain and to keep the pounds off. Have you ever heard the expression, "You are what you eat"? Well, it's true! Here's what he experts say…

Sugar is the number one dietary component to consume the least. Sugar is stored as fat, and is one of the most difficult energy stores to get through burning off. Even pure fat (if low in saturated fat) is easier to burn off than sugar. Additionally, though sugar may give you a perceived "energy spike," it comes with a crash that will deplete your energy and de-motivate you in the long run. Keep it in small doses, you need not change your entire diet drastically to start with. However, cut a serving of sweets out each day, or add less sugar to your coffee and tea. Once you start lowering your sugar intake, you'll see the difference!

Instead, stick to proteins and lean meats. Fish, lean ground beef, turkey and chicken will be your best options as they are rich in protein and are easily converted to energy by your body. Another way to get protein is through yogurt and nuts (though nuts are higher in fat than the previously mentioned foods). Again, no need for a drastic diet change, but maybe instead of having those cookies or that cupcake, swap it for a snack higher in protein like a cup of yogurt or a trail mix bar. You can even have more of these foods and feel fuller, as they are almost all free of sugar and carbohydrates (a more complex version of sugar). The best part about adding protein to your diet? You'll add muscle while keeping the extra weight off *and* be able to stay on the go!

Time Management

Another way to get the most out of your energy spike is planning the best time to do your yoga. It is ideal to wake up and start in the morning, as it boosts your energy for the day. Don't have time or can't commit to the early morning hours? Give it a shot after work or in the afternoon, right around the time you might be so inclined to take a nap, and you'll find you'd rather get up and be productive than lay down for a bit of some sleep.

Energy + Yoga = More Energy

Energy is used up when you move or simply when your body is carrying out its natural functions, and in the process, it creates even *more* energy. This means that if you stick to a routine of yoga as your light exercise, the more energy you burn, the more energized you will feel in turn. The amazing new surges and stores of energy you're feeling come from the release of energy and endorphins that come from moving your body in a precise, deliberate and concentrated way. This feeling can go a long way when your schedule is busy, filled with a heavy workload, friend and family obligations, and down time.

It's hard not to feel tired now and then! It will take some time, but learning to use these short poses for the minimum time when you're feeling depleted will make a world of difference for your mood, mental health, stress levels, and energy levels. The best part about using yoga for weight loss and conserving energy is that it doesn't take the amount of time and effort as rigorous workouts, yet it brings all of the same benefits. It may require a little more patience, but the results will be well worthwhile. Big changes are on the way, so be ready to embrace them!

Get Ready – The New You Is Just Around the Corner!

You may find that while incorporating these small changes into your life, you'll feel differently. Having more energy allows you to do more, feeling more productive and furthermore, happier. Eating even a little better by replacing one snack a day will slowly reduce your calorie intake, and you'll steadily see the changes in your body while you make a habit out of using yoga. This makes for an overall change, what we call, a "transformation."

Embrace these changes! It doesn't happen overnight, but if you can recognize and further each accomplishment you make, you will find it easier to stay determined and stick with the new routine you've built for yourself. If you brought yourself here to read this EBook, you're already halfway there. You're interested, and by learning as much as you can and starting out at a reasonable pace, you can keep going even when the going gets tough!

At The End of the Day…

Yoga's many benefits have touched the lives of millions across the world. Even they had to start somewhere, and your journey can start right now. Don't miss the opportunity to use a simple tactic to change your life, lose that extra weight, and stay focused during the day. Once you see the results, you'll want to stick to it for life!

Don't forget, yoga is about concentration, calm, and stability. Don't fret that you're not getting an intense workout like you might for exercise, and don't get down on yourself if now and then, you really need to nap, and choose to do the yoga later at a stressful time when you need to unwind.

Pace yourself. Don't forget, any transformation is about you, so make it happen for *yourself*!

Hatha Yoga Poses In Order Of Progression

The main goal of Hatha Yoga is much the same as other forms of yoga practice. It attempts to blend the spirit of the individual with the greater spirit of the universe, improving the health of the spirit, mind, body and emotions. Hatha Yoga has been said to help practitioners attain inner peace and a feeling of oneness with the universe. Remember that no matter what type of yoga you choose to perform, concentration is a very important factor.

All types of yoga have some similarities. However, they differ in methods or intent in other areas. Hatha Yoga's main focus is the preparation of the body, so that the spirit will be able to perform its function in bringing the practitioner to enlightenment. A great deal of confusion can arise, as many people don't realize that it's important to have a healthy, fit body in order to successfully attain spiritual enlightenment.

Hatha Yoga practice is applied to the body in order to strengthen it and the spirit inside. Its physical techniques are often used by people who aren't interested in spiritual advancement, but who would like to receive the physical benefits of Hatha Yoga as well. This is the most commonly taught form of yoga, and is thus the type that comes to most people's minds when yoga is mentioned. Other styles of yoga, some of which are derived from Hatha Yoga, include Kundalini, Bikram, Ashtanga, and Power Yoga.

In addition to the physical benefits of Hatha Yoga, there are also mental ones. It's been said to assist in the development of greater concentration and focusing abilities, in addition to reducing stress and anxiety. For many people, this is an important benefit, and something they need in their lives. If you're being distracted and need some time to relax, Hatha Yoga might be the right solution.

For those who are looking for a spiritual benefit, Hatha Yoga allows you to find your own divine light. It can help you become stronger, more flexible, and more relaxed. Performing Hatha Yoga allows the energy of your spirit to flow more freely, since the mind, spirit, and body are more closely in harmony. If your body is weakened, this weakness also affects the mind and spirit. Skeptical? Consider how hard it is to concentrate when you have a headache.

Practicing Hatha Yoga can help you cope with stress, and can relieve some of your tension and pain. If work is leaving you exhausted, you need to find time to relax and rejuvenate yourself. Hatha Yoga is an excellent remedy, that can help you release built up worries and anxiety.

70 Yoga Hatha Poses (Asanas) for less stress, anxiety and weight loss

The following is an entire hatha flow sequence of beneficial hatha yoga poses. Each pose is pictured in the finish movement of each pose. Just click on the image to proceed further to a professionally narrated video of each of the asanas. If the video doesn't load in a new browser window, click on the link below the image. Each asana is numbered in the order of their progression. It should be noted that each is explained in detail by a professional narrator, and is easy enough for anyone to do, especially the yoga beginner.

Click For Video Demonstration => Click for the video 01 Childs Pose

Click For Video Demonstration => 02 Hamstring Stretch Right

Click For Video Demonstration => 03 Hamstring Stretch Left

Click For Video Demonstration => 04 Cat Cow Pose

Click For Video Demonstration => 05 Downward Dog

Click For Video Demonstration => 06 Beginner High Plank

Click For Video Demonstration => 07 High Plank

Click For Video Demonstration => 08 Chaturunga

Click For Video Demonstration => 09 Cobra Upward Facing Dog

10 Beginners Flow

Click For Video Demonstration => 10 Beginners Flow

11 flow 2

Click For Video Demonstration => 11 flow 2

Click For Video Demonstration => 12 Low Runners Lunge Left

Click For Video Demonstration => 13 Low Lunge Right Side

Click For Video Demonstration => 14 High Lunge Left

Click For Video Demonstration => 15 High Lunge Right

Click For Video Demonstration => 16 Warrior One Left

Click For Video Demonstration => 17 Warrior Right

Click For Video Demonstration => 18 Warrior Two Left

Click For Video Demonstration => 19 Warrior Two Right

Click For Video Demonstration => 20 Standing Forward Bend

Click For Video Demonstration => 21 Chair Pose Side

Click For Video Demonstration => 22 Chair Pose Front

Click For Video Demonstration => 23 Chair Pose Twist Left

Click For Video Demonstration => 24 Chair Pose Twist Right

Click For Video Demonstration => 25 Triangle Left

Click For Video Demonstration => 26 Triangle Right

Click For Video Demonstration => 27 Reverse Warrior Pose Left

Click For Video Demonstration => 28 Reverse Warrior Pose

Click For Video Demonstration => 29 Half Moon Left

Click For Video Demonstration => 30 Half Moon Right

Click For Video Demonstration => 31 Extended Side Angle Left 1

Click For Video Demonstration => 32 Extended Side Angle Right

33 Revolved Side Angle Pose

Click For Video Demonstration => 33 Revolved Side Angle Pose

Click For Video Demonstration => 34 Revolved Side Angle Right

Click For Video Demonstration => 35 Warrior Three Left

Click For Video Demonstration => <u>37 Humble Warrior Left Side</u>

38 Humble Warrior Right Side

Click For Video Demonstration => 38 Humble Warrior Right Side

Click For Video Demonstration => 39 Prayer Twist Left Side

Click For Video Demonstration => 40 Prayer Twist Right Side

41 Wide Legged Forward Bend

Click For Video Demonstration => 41 Wide Legged Forward Bend

Click For Video Demonstration => 42 Side Plank Left Side

Click For Video Demonstration => 43 Side Plank Right Side

Click For Video Demonstration => 44 Three Legged Dog Left

Click For Video Demonstration => 47 Tree Pose Right Side

Click For Video Demonstration => 48 Eagle Pose Left Side

49 Eagle Pose Right Side

Click For Video Demonstration => 50 Dancers Pose Front View

Click For Video Demonstration => 51 Dancers Pose Right Side

Click For Video Demonstration => 52 Camel Pose

Click For Video Demonstration => 53 Fire Log Left Side

Click For Video Demonstration => 54 Fire Log Right Side

Click For Video Demonstration => 55 Seated Twist Left Side

Click For Video Demonstration => 56 Seated Twist Right Side

Click For Video Demonstration => 57 Pigeon Pose Left Side

Click For Video Demonstration => 58 Pigeon Right Side

59 Seated Forward Bend

Click For Video Demonstration => 59 Seated Forward Bend

Click For Video Demonstration => 60 Cobblers Pose

Click For Video Demonstration => 61 Revolved Head To Knee Stretch Left

Click For Video Demonstration => 62 Revolved Head To Knee Right Side

Click For Video Demonstration => 63 Thread The Needle Left

Click For Video Demonstration => 64 Thread The Needle Right Side

Click For Video Demonstration => 65 Bridge Pose

Click For Video Demonstration => 66 Happy Baby

Click For Video Demonstration => 67 Laying Twist Left

Click For Video Demonstration => 68 Laying Twist Right Side

Click For Video Demonstration => 69 Shavasana Pose

70 Namaste

Click For Video Demonstration => <u>70 Namaste</u>

Conclusion

Thank you again for downloading this book!

I hope this book was able to help you to discover the benefits using yoga for weight loss, added energy in your daily life, and guiding you towards a new you! Don't forget to use this EBook as a reference if ever you should need to check back on any information.

The next step is to explore how yoga will fit into your life, look to find the benefits for yourself and your life, and use your new knowledge and skill to be a life-long yoga participant for further transforming your life.

Finally, if you enjoyed this book, then I'd like to ask you for a favor, would you be kind enough to leave a review for this book on Amazon? It ' d be greatly appreciated!

Click here to leave a review for this book on Amazon!

Raise your life, raise your vibration!

Daniel Amos

Tranquility Transformation

Meditation Fast Start Guide To Lose Weight, Create Amazing Abundance and Live Stress Free Effortlessly

Daniel Amos

Introduction: Why Meditate…

So... here you are.

And, since you're already here, reading this, I probably don't need to convince you about the reasons or benefits of meditating.

But, just in case you need a few more reasons, or a friendly reminder, here are just some of the benefits...

Meditation can help you to:

- reduce stress and be more relaxed, therefore enjoy life more,
- achieve more mental clarity, better memory and recall,
- increase creativity and improve problem-solving ability
- bring your body into balance, improve overall health, normalize blood pressure, etc.
- improve your overall physical appearance, skin tone, muscle relaxation, etc.
- be (and appear) more confident, calm, and thus in control

...and lots more wonderful stuff.

And, if you're interested in going a little deeper, meditation can also help you to become more in touch with who you *really* are.

In other words, it can help you *find and know who you really are*. Not what the world has told you - or is telling you - that you are... or what others think, believe or want you to be. But, who you really, truly are.

You get to connect with your essence. And, as such, you start to align more with your true purpose, and with life itself.

But, that's only if you're interested in that sort of thing. ;-)

Ultimately, you don't really need a reason to meditate. Or rather, you *shouldn't* need a reason.

However, if a reason is what you need to *motivate* you to do it regularly, so that you can enjoy all the amazing benefits, then that's just fine. Nothing wrong with that at all.

The most important thing is that you start meditating.

Who Can Actually Benefit From Meditation

Who is meditation really for? And who can benefit from doing it?

Well, *everybody*... but, especially those people who think that they *don't have time* to meditate. The busier and crazier your life is, the more vital it is for you to start meditating.

Oh, by the way... if your blood pressure is extremely low during your normal waking state, you may want to check with your physician first, before you introduce meditation into your lifestyle.)

Otherwise, anybody and everybody can benefit from this practice.

It doesn't matter whether you're religious or not... or whether you're an athiest, agnostic, spiritual, scientific, Amish, Buddhist, realist, optimist, or any other -ist, -ic, or -ish.

The practice of meditation cannot, should not, and will not interfere with - nor complicate - your current beliefs.

The reason is simple: mediation is not about *believing* anything. It's simply a practice.

It's a practice of just being. (It's not about believing or even thinking, really...as you'll soon find out.)

Most of our life is such that it only involves the 'human' part of who we are.

Meditation can help you to give a little of your time to the 'being' part of the 'human being' that you are. So, it's really about bringing balance into your life.

One final thought before we continue...

I would *highly* recommend that you read this entire report - from start to finish - at least once, before trying to practice anything that's shared in here. That way, you will be sure that you're not missing any of the important pieces of the process nor the spirit of the practice itself.

Common Problems and Obstacles

So, you already know that you should be meditating, especially if you tend to have a busy, hectic or crazy life.

But, for some reason, you are not able to do it regularly - if at all.

Let's discuss why most people don't or can't meditate, despite their best efforts.

Some of the most common reasons people don't or cannot meditate regularly, or never even start, are:

- They don't have time.
- They don't know how.
- They do know how but they're not sure if they're doing it correctly.
- They're not sure which technique/method is the best one for them.
- They are not able to "clear their mind".
- They don't know what to expect, or what they should be experiencing during the session.
- They can't seem to hold their focus (or do the process) for too long.
- They can't sit still, or their bodies can't handle the stress, strain, or pain.

...or some other valid reason. (There are many of them.)

We will address each of the above problems individually. And, we'll discuss how we can resolve them so that you can be on your way to meditating like a master monk, in the quickest and easiest way possible.

If you pay attention to the tips and advice I share in this report, you'll get more out your mediation – and go much deeper – much, much sooner than most people ever will.

The "I Don't Have Time" Dilemma

If you don't have time to meditate because your life is too busy, cluttered, or chaotic, then you absolutely **must** start meditating.

(Don't worry, I will show you how, even if you don't have time. :-)

And, if you don't start soon, things will only get worse, and they will continue to spin out of control until it's too late to fix most of the problems, because the damage will have already been done.

First of all, you should know that sitting down *formally* (and closing your eyes) to meditate for an hour, 30 minutes or even **5** minutes is **not** necessary...nor is it the only way to meditate.

I will show you how to start meditating *during* your regular day - without closing your eyes, while you're out and about... taking care of business, grocery shopping, or even having lunch.

The most important thing for you to realize right now is that time is insignificant and even irrelevant. This may seem to conflict with what most meditation teachers say or teach, but it's true. (I will build on this "time" concept soon, in a later chapter.)

You can meditate for one hour or you can meditate for one *second*. When you do it the way I'll show you to, time simply won't be an issue anymore. (And you'll still enjoy the benefits that come from meditating.)

I know that the above statements may seem a bit confusing or unorthodox
right now, but all of it will soon start to make a lot of sense.

For now, just realize that "not having time" will not be a problem for you
anymore. :-)

Not Knowing *How* to Meditate

There are a lot of meditation techniques and schools of thought out there. Some are simple, others are incredibly complex.

Some can take as little as 10 minutes to learn and start practicing...and others require a minimum of 5 (and up to 10) *days* of complete isolation from civilization, just to be able to learn to start *practicing* in the correct way. (That's not how long it takes to *master* it, mind you. It takes that long *just* to learn to do it *right*.)

Ultimately, all forms of meditation are designed to take you to the same place. It doesn't really matter if you choose to take the longest, most complex road...or the simplest and easiest one.

There are people out there who try to learn one new meditation technique each week. (There are also people who try to complicate their life more than it really is or needs to be. ;-)

And, learning about several kinds of mediation is fine if you're the curious or investigative type.

Unfortunately, many people learn dozens of different techniques just so they can feel good about themselves, or about knowing more than *others*.

Many of these individuals are the same ones who are constantly talking - and telling others - about what new and "fascinating" meditation technique they have just learned this week.

Sadly, many of these people never really learn to meditate - and thus, never get to enjoy the benefits of meditating - because, somewhere along the line (without them realizing,) their goal shifted from learning to "collecting meditation *techniques*" and/or to turn it into the "having more" game.

It's not about how many different techniques you can learn. Because you only need one.

During my research over the years, I have come to learn several of them. But, I almost always use only *one*.

And, if you happen to be one of those individuals who doesn't have much time to do the formal "sit down" mediation, *then* you can learn one or two more techniques (as I mentioned earlier) because you actually have a valid reason to do so.

But, that's about it. This isn't a competition to see who can learn (or collect/acquire) the most number of techniques and styles of meditation.

Meditation's Main Purpose and How This Will Literally Change Your Life Instantly

One could say that the main purpose of meditation is to cut down on the mental noise and inner dialogue...the continuous mental static that exists in your mind...that prevents you from touching a deeper and more intelligent place inside you. (We will go with that basic explanation, for now.)

This place inside you is where you can go to recharge your body, mind and spirit... to spark inspiration and creativity...to simply gain peace of mind... or to experience many other benefits.

As, I mentioned earlier, it doesn't matter *why* you go to that place, how you get there, or even **when** you get there... just that you go.

The simplest and easiest way to get there is to create an atmosphere around you that *allows* you to access that deeper place inside.

Contrary to what most people believe, this atmosphere can be created almost **anywhere**. You can create it in the privacy of your own home or even in the middle of a busy shopping mall. (More on that later.)

Obviously, I would suggest that you start at home, where you can find privacy and a quiet place, so you can learn to focus on just the process, for now, without any outside distractions.

But, if that's not possible for you...or even if you don't think you have the time to do so, that's okay. We will talk about the alternative method, in a later section of this report.

Alright... so what is the simplest and easiest way to meditate, if you *do* have the time and place to do so?

How to Meditate: Secrets Revealed *The Simplest and Easiest Method*

So... once you have found a quiet place, with enough privacy for you to sit down for at least 5 to 10 minutes, the best way to start meditating is to...

1. Sit comfortably. It doesn't matter where. You can be on the floor, on a chair, on your favorite couch, or even on the edge of your bed. (Lying down is not recommended. You will see why, soon.)

If you don't have a private area to call your own, you could simply lock yourself in the bathroom for a few minutes. (The location doesn't matter.)

2. Close your eyes and gently start to become aware of your environment.

You may hear some sounds/noises (the ticking of a clock, voices coming from outside or nearby, birds chirping, dogs barking, etc.) You may smell something (flowers, perfume, deodorant, shampoo, etc. in your room, on you, or even something coming from outside your room.)

You may even sense vibrations or movement (from traffic, train, airplane... people walking outside or around your building, etc.)

Don't try to search for or reach out your attention out there to find stuff to pay attention to. Simply become aware of what naturally comes to you. And, if you only feel silence, that's wonderful.

And, try not to judge, identify or label any of the sounds or sensations either. Just let them do what they're doing, without feeling the need or wish that any of those things should change so that you could meditate better. Just let everything be as it is.

Focus on those external sounds and sensations for a minute or two.

3. Next, gently bring your attention inwards...to your body... and start paying attention to what's going on in your body, now... just as you did with your surroundings earlier.

Notice what's going on in your body...without judging, labeling or analyzing anything.

You may notice that certain areas are tighter than others. You may become aware of a little pain or pressure here and there. You may even become aware of how your body is resting against the surface of the chair, couch, etc.

Sometimes, you may also become aware of your heart beat and/or your pulse (either around your temples, wrists, or both.)

Again, simply observe what's going on in your body, without judging, remembering why, or needing to change anything (including any pain or tightness.) Just let them all be, as they are. And, just relax into it all.

4. Finally, bring your attention gently to your breathing. (You may have already become aware of your breathing in Step 3 above. If that's the case, that's just fine.)

In this step, simply observe your breathing... without interfering with it, i.e. without consciously trying to breathe in and out yourself, and without wanting to speed up or slow down the breathing rate. Just let your body breathe on it's own.

If you're not able to let it happen on it's own, and are pulled into controlling the breaths yourself, that okay. Don't fight or resist that either.

Just observe what's going on, even if the 'what' includes your own tendencies. Let all of it happen, without analyzing or needing it to be different.

5. Continue to observe your breaths without interfering with the rhythm (if you can.)

You may notice that your breathing may change rhythm on it's own, occasionally. It may become faster or slower... or deeper or shallower.

Whatever it does on it's own, just let it be. Simply observe.

After several automatic breaths, you may notice your body becoming lighter and more relaxed. And, if this doesn't happen, that's just fine too.

Remember, don't try to force or wish for anything to happen. Your only job right now is to just observe. That's all.

Stay in this observation state for as long as you're able to. If it's 10 minutes, that's fine. If it's 5 minutes, that's fine too. And, even if it's just one or two minutes, that's also fine.

Just stay with for as long as you comfortably can, without forcing yourself, and keep observing what's going on. Nothing else needs to be done here.

6. Whenever you feel like stopping the process, give yourself several seconds (and up to 30 seconds, or more, if needed) and gently open your eyes again.

Stay sitting for just a little bit, if you can, and just **be**.

Now, if you feel like getting up, you can. Do whatever you'd like, whether it's stretching, going to the restroom, getting a drink of water, walking around a bit, stepping out for some air, or whatever.

You are done for now.

If this happens to be your first time doing this, congratulate yourself! You just did your first meditation session!

Did You Do It Correctly?

Most people will often start questioning or wondering about certain things immediately after they have finished meditating. Many of them will start wondering and questioning even while they're right in the *middle* of meditating.

Common questions like these will come to their - and maybe your - mind...

"Did I do what I was supposed to do?" (after they have just finished meditating.)

...Or...

"Am I doing this correctly?" (while they are in the middle of meditating.)

The simple answer to all of those types of questions is... **YES**.

You did just what you were supposed to do, and you did it exactly as you were supposed to do it, *in that moment in time.*

Another way to look at it is, none of those things (or questions) matter.

Think of it this way...

If you're hungry, it doesn't matter whether you eat your food with a fork, a spoon, a straw, with your hands, or any other way.

The important thing is that you do eat.

How you got the food into your mouth, which angle or direction from which you delivered the food to your mouth, which hand you used, which way you were facing, or any other such details do not matter at all.

In other words, don't worry about any of that stuff. Just be happy with the fact that *you did meditate.*

That's the only thing that matters. (All of this stuff will make more and more sense as you read through the rest of the sections below.)

The Hard Facts: What You Should Expect

This is another common (and valid) question that will come into most people's mind...during, before, or even after their meditation session...

"What should I expect to see, feel, or experience while I am meditating?"

The short answer is, do not expect *anything specific* to happen. Because, there is no right or wrong experience.

And, if you start to wonder about, search for, or expect something specific/significant to happen, then you will be focusing on *that* instead of just observing.

In other words, if you start looking for something in particular, you will miss whatever else that *is* happening. Even if it's nothing. (You won't even be able to experience nothing, because you'll be searching or expecting "something.")

So, the main idea, as shared earlier, is to simply observe... without judging, labeling, analyzing, or even searching nor expecting for anything in particular to happen.

Just be there as an observer. Without looking for anything. Simply notice what is happening - even if *nothing* is happening.

Having said that, here are the three most common things that *could* happen...

1. As you're paying attention to your breath, and to whatever else is going on,

you *may* find your mind wandering. Certain thoughts may arise in your head. And, that's okay.

...OR...

2. As you're paying attention to your breath, and whatever else, you may gently fall into a quiet, peaceful space where you're simply *being*...and quietly observing.

...OR...

3. You may fall asleep.

Again, there are no right or wrong experiences. There are just experiences. And all of them are perfectly normal/valid experiences.

However, if you find yourself falling asleep during meditation (which you will only realize when you wake back up,) that's okay. It simply means that your body needed the rest.

If this keeps happening each time you try to meditate, it may be a sign that you're not getting enough rest during your regular sleeping schedule, for whatever reason.

So, you may want to look into that and try to remedy it, so you can find a way to get your body enough rest.

If, during your meditation, you notice that your mind starts to wander after a while, and you become distracted with thoughts, that's okay. We will discuss that further, in later sections of the report.

Lastly, there is a chance that you may realize you weren't the most comfortable in the position or location where you meditated.

If that's the case, you can try to adjust accordingly.

If your clothes were too tight, wear looser ones next time. If your chair or couch wasn't very comfortable, you could try padding it or using something else to sit on.

If your body was starting to feel fatigued, strained or in pain, you could (again) try adjusting and accommodating for that (stretching and/or relaxing prior to meditating, or whatever else works.)

(And, yes, you are allowed to adjust and/or move around a bit, while you're in the middle of meditating. Just do your best to not move around too much or too often.)

How Long Should You Meditate?

While there is no set amount of time that is ideal for meditating, the most commonly *suggested* time range is about 15 to 30 minutes.

But, remember what I stated earlier, the amount of time is ultimately irrelevant. And, I'll explain why soon.

However, when you're starting out, you can have a loose time goal in mind. And, you could either notice the time before you start, or even set an alarm to alert you after a certain number of minutes.

You could do 5-minute sessions twice per day, for the first week. During the second week, you could try to shoot for 10 minutes per session, twice per day.

Ideally, you would want to start/conduct your meditations during the same time, every day, but it's not a big deal if you're not always able to do that.

Just do your best to keep a scheduled time set aside, twice each day, for meditating.

And, if you aren't able to stick to the scheduled time occasionally, don't beat yourself up over it. Just reschedule it for an earlier or later spot in the day.

Ultimately, the length of time is not that important. (You shouldn't make your goal or pursuit to be able to meditate longer than before, or longer than others.)

So, if you are only able to sit in silence for one minute, or even for one second, that's still much better than not meditating at all.

Just keep practicing. And, don't pay much attention to your mind (or your ego) trying to make you feel bad about not being able to meditate for longer than you are currently doing.

As I mentioned earlier, this is not a competition (not with others nor with your own self.)

What's the Best Time(s) to Meditate?

Again, there is no hard and fast rule as to what particular time you should meditate. However, ideally, you would want to...

1. Meditate as early in the morning as possible... immediately after you wake up, use the restroom and have a cup of water. (Warm water is recommended.)

...and...

2. Just before you go to bed at night.

Whichever two times you choose to meditate in the day, try to meditate every day at those same two times, i.e. keep the same schedule daily, as best as you can.

And, if something comes up where you have to adjust your schedules a bit, that's fine. Don't worry too much about it.

And, definitely do *not* stress out about it. Stress and meditation are just not meant to go together, for any reason.

If you ever catch yourself stressing about anything related to your meditation, either remedy the situation quickly or let it go and move on.

The important thing is that you do your best *to* meditate. The exact time is not extremely important.

Life can be unpredictable, and schedules tend to change sometimes. Also, on some days, you may have to get up earlier or go to bed earlier (or even later.) So, adjust accordingly. And, don't worry about it.

Similarly, if you happen to experience one of those days where you just can't find a way to meditate two times, it's not the end of the world. Just do your best to either do one later or earlier in that same day, i.e. sometime in the afternoon, mid-morning, etc. Or just make up for it sometime later in the week.

The "Clear Your Mind" Syndrome

At some point during their meditative journey, almost everyone encounters the dreaded "mind." And, even before they ever start meditating, most people are cautioned, warned, or instructed to "clear your mind."

It took me almost 15 years to finally figure out that meditating has *nothing* to do with trying to "clear your mind."

Unfortunately, most newcomers are still being advised/instructed/told to clear their mind, or quiet the mental noise, in order to be able to meditate successfully.

The truly unfortunate part is, even most of the long-time meditation practitioners out there - who have been practicing for *a decade or two* - are still trying to "clear their mind"...without much success. (This includes many of the **instructors**, too!)

Most people, including many instructors and teachers, end up turning the mind into an *enemy* that they have to fight against, resist, or try to shut down. That is the exact *opposite* of what you should be doing.

Yes, I am aware that (earlier in this very report,) I myself stated the purpose of meditation to be about "cutting down on the mental noise and inner dialogue" so you can access that deeper place inside yourself.

However, your primary focus should not be to "clear your mind" because doing so is almost impossible, especially if you focus directly on that task.

Of course, if you are able to quiet your mind, that's wonderful. But, don't waste your time on *trying* to do that.

The mind is such a thing that the more you try to quiet it, the more you try to resist its thoughts, the more prevalent and persistent it gets.

Besides, meditation is not about fighting, resisting, or even "trying" to do anything.

As I mentioned earlier, in the "***How to Meditate***" section, your only job during meditation is to observe. Without the need to judge, label, analyze, or change anything.

When you let go of the need (or desire) to judge, label or analyze, a good amount of mental noise and ego simply dissolves.

Not all of it goes away, mind you. A good amount of mind chatter and inner dialogue still remains. And, in the next section, I'll show you how to masterfully handle that situation.

The Real Question: But, What About the Mental Noise?

In this section, I am going to reveal the most powerful secret, and a few cool tricks, that can help you become a master-level meditation expert in the shortest amount of time possible.

Of course, the purpose is not to "get" it sooner than others, nor is it to brag about being an expert to others. It is simply about being able to start enjoying the amazing benefits of meditation as soon as possible.

At any rate, let's talk about how to handle one of the most common challenges that every beginner meditator - and even most veteran meditators - have to deal with.

Almost immediately after you start meditating, you will find your mind beginning to wander off. Certain thoughts will arise, and before you realize it, you will be lost in thought.

Sometimes, you may catch yourself quickly. And, other times, 30 minutes or more may pass before you realize that you have been thinking about *everything* on the planet...except for the one thing you should be...which is to meditate, i.e. to simply observe.

So, how do you stop the mind from wandering? How do you stop the endless thought stream that comes flooding in, the moment you close your eyes and try to be still?

The big secret is to start observing your thoughts as well!

Yes, it's as simple as that.

The concept of observing your own thoughts may seem a bit weird at first, but it's actually quite simple...and brilliant.

So...instead of trying to *not* think about anything...or to clear your mind...or to resist or fight your mind, you can actually start to *watch* your thoughts.

You see, most of us are so caught up in our thoughts all the time, we start thinking and believing that *we are our thoughts*. And, many of us also believe that we are our minds. That we and our mind are one.

But that is not the case. You are not your mind, and you are certainly not your thoughts.

You are the *awareness* underneath your mind and your thoughts.

And, when you start to really *become aware* of the fact that you *are* the awareness itself, instead of the mind, that is the beginning of the powerful and all-important **separation** between you and your mind.

That is the beginning of *freedom* from your mind, and from being lost in thought all the time.

Our lives are run by our thoughts and our mind. The mind just does not shut up. It is always questioning, analyzing, tearing apart, labeling, and of course judging everything!

And, we as humans have started to believe that it's a good thing! We pride ourselves in how quickly our minds can analyze, label and judge things, situations, and especially other people.

Many of us have even made successful careers out of judging everything and everyone.

It's sad really. Because the more we label, analyze and judge, the more we separate and isolate ourselves from everything and everyone around us.

Wars between nations are started this way.

But, our planet is starting to awaken. Our species is also slowly waking up. And, that's one of the reasons meditation is so important.

So, how do we observe our mind and our thoughts?

We don't do it by fighting or resisting it. We do it by *allowing* it to be. We give up the need to change what the mind is doing, which is what it always does: *think thoughts.*

And, by allowing our mind to do what it loves to do, and by simply observing each new thought as it comes into our mind, we take their power away. Because what you resist will only persist.

So, by allowing each new thought to come floating in freely, and simply observing what that thought is, we get out of it's way so that it can continue floating *out* and away, just as easily as it came in.

It's so simple that it hurts! :-)

As soon as you see a new thought pop into your mind, you could get the feeling of... "Ah, there's another thought. And, this one is about the bills I have to pay. Okay, I will let this thought be, without interfering with it, and just observe. Let's see what's next..."

Of course, you won't be saying those words nor thinking those words specifically. But, that is what your feeling and sense will be as you observe each new thought float in.

Simply observe and let it be. Don't judge, don't analyze, and definitely don't resist. Just watch each thought float away just as easily as it came in.

As you start to do this, you will keep taking your mind's power away because you won't be resisting it anymore. (The more you resist and fight it, the more power it gets.)

And as you continue to do this, while you're meditating, you will notice fewer and fewer thoughts coming in.

And, very soon after, you will get to that deeper space of quiet... calm... stillness.

That's where magic happens.

But remember, don't *try* to go there. Don't hope to go there. And, definitely don't expect to go there. Those are all ways to *guarantee* that you'll *never* get there.

So, don't worry about whether you'll get there on the first try, or even the 10th try. Wanting to get there will only cloud the path.

The only way to get there is to just be...and observe anything (or nothing) as it unfolds during your meditative practice.

And, the more you do that, the more you practice just observing and just *being*, the more stillness you will experience...and the deeper you will go.

But, even during all of these deeper states, remember to not do anything. Don't become anxious, don't even start looking for or trying to define/label the stillness. That will only activate your mind again. And the thoughts will start coming all over again.

Remember to just be. Just enjoy what **is**.

Don't expect anything...and you will get to see everything (which is nothing, i.e. the stillness.) Simply by allowing it to be.

Practice entering this space of stillness often. Spend as much time as you can in there. And, enjoy all the wonderful benefits it will continue to provide you with.

One Of The Biggest Challenges Conquered: The Question of "Time"

One of the challenges that I mentioned earlier in the report was the "*I Don't Have Time*" dilemma.

And, I had alluded to the idea that ultimately "time is irrelevant" when meditation is concerned.

Also, I had promised to show you how to start meditating *during* your regular day, if sitting down *formally* (and closing your eyes) to meditate was not an option for you.

I had mentioned that you could meditate for one hour or for one *second*. When done the way I'd show you, time wouldn't matter.

And, finally I had advised that if you didn't have time to meditate because your life is too busy, cluttered, or chaotic, then you absolutely **had** to start meditating.

So... let's discuss this further. And, I'll also share one more meditation technique that will address the "I don't have time" issue.

Firstly, I keep stating that "time" is irrelevant or unimportant in meditation. And, the reason is simple...

The length of time doesn't matter because the space of stillness itself that you're entering during meditation is <u>timeless</u>. Time does not exist there.

Nor does it have a location or an address. You cannot point or lead anyone there. Not even yourself. That is why you can only get there when you become still yourself. And, that's when the stillness inside you reveals itself.

Now, let's discuss the alternative meditation method you can use if you don't have time, space nor privacy to sit down for a formal meditation...

I call this method the "waking meditation" (there may be other names for it out there) and you can do this just about anywhere, as you go about your day.

If a scheduled, sit-down meditation done twice per day is not possible for you, the "waking meditation" is the next best thing. (In fact, I would recommend that you occasionally practice this form of meditation *even if* you are doing the formal sit-down daily meditation.)

The way to do this meditation technique is to simply bring awareness into whatever it is you're doing during your waking state.

You would focus your full attention on the task at hand, no matter how simple or mundane the task happened to be....and you would be *fully present* while doing it.

You can only be fully present if you're **not** thinking about what you're doing.

You're not wondering about why you're doing it, you're not analyzing the process by which it is being done, you're not judging the process nor anything or anyone that did this process before you... none of that.

Because, if you're *thinking* about what you're doing, or how you're doing, than you're not really giving the task at hand your full attention.

Also, you wouldn't be thinking about other non-related things either...whether it's about what else you have to do, what you've already done, what the weather would be like, what you're going to eat after doing this, or what your pet must be doing right now, etc. etc. None of that either.

And again, understand that it's **not** about *forcing* yourself to *not* think about other stuff. That would be fighting with or resisting the mind. And, you already know that doing so doesn't work.

So, you simply focus your attention on whatever is in front of you right now. That's all. And, you don't even judge, analyze or label that in any way either.

And, by the process of being fully present in what you were doing, you would start to create a spaciousness around you that would be very similar to the stillness that the sit-down meditation would bring you to.

You could do this in the office, while out grocery shopping or even before you leave your home.

At home, you could do this while you brush your teeth, floss, shave, or shower. And, you would simply bring your full attention to whatever it is you were doing...whether it was moving the brush against your teeth, focusing on how the razor felt against your skin while you carefully moved it, lathering your hair or body, or feeling the water falling against your skin and body.

You could even do it when you were having breakfast, lunch, a snack, or dinner... by simply enjoying the food completely, and even fully focusing on the process of eating.

(People who start eating in this conscious way find incredibly more enjoyment from eating, they feel satiated sooner, and they usually end up eating **less**...because they also start focusing on how their body is feeling during - and after - eating something.)

If you were at the office, shredding paper, you would allow your mind to focus fully on just the task of shredding paper instead of thinking about how the paper shredder works, or who invented the shredder. And, you wouldn't even be thinking about who used the shredder before you and whether they were the ones who left it so messy, or whatever else that may come to your mind.

If any of those thoughts do pop up in your head, simply smile knowing that you already read about it in this report...or that you already *knew* you'd encounter some of those thoughts.

And then, gently come back to the act of "shredding paper"... of picking up the paper, bringing it up to the shredder, pushing it through the teeth/blades, and watching it being ripped to shreds.

If you were taking the elevator to another floor, you would push the elevator button, observe the elevator door close, and then you would enjoy the silence instead of wanting to get to your desired floor quicker. Wanting to get there quicker will not make the elevator go faster. So, instead of wanting to be at your destination already, you might as well enjoy the few moments of peace and quiet in your day, during your elevator ride.

If you were taking a break, you would simply take a break. You would *not* try to make phone calls, or send text messages, or any of that stuff. You would simply sit down (or stand) somewhere and just *be*. Be there fully. Have your full attention and focus right where you are instead of being lost in thought. Look around, enjoy your environment - or at least become aware of what's going on around you - without needing to have opinions or thoughts about it.

If you were driving your vehicle, you would be completely focused just on the process of driving. You would become aware of the little steps you are taking in order to drive, and you would also become more aware of your surroundings. You would shut off the radio or stereo and simply focus on the process of driving, with all of your attention and awareness.

If you came to a red light, you would enjoy the few seconds of stillness, again without needing to get to where you were going any quicker.

With a little practice, you will be able to feel and sense the underlying stillness anywhere, at any time. Even if you're in the middle of chaos. And, that's kind of the point of this practice (to be able to be still - or "meditate" - while you're awake and out of your quiet, private space.)

And, you would do so even while you hear children yelling/crying, dogs barking, plates crashing to the floor, or sirens screeching outside... you will be able to let all of those things just be as they are, and notice (or become *aware*) of the stillness in which all of that stuff happens.

So, in the end, what you're *really* doing is becoming aware of the stillness outside of you (in the physical world) by becoming aware of - and connecting with - that place of stillness *inside* of you. That's the secret to this waking meditation.

If all of that sounds weird right now, that's okay. Just start by practicing this waking meditation during the quieter or calmer moments of your life, first. :-

) And gradually try to work on those other busier or noisier moments.

These little moments of being fully present in what you're doing - or just being still and aware, wherever you are - may not seem very significant to you right now, but believe me, they are very powerful and very transformative.

And, the more you start to bring tiny bits of awareness and presence into your life, as often as you can during any given day, the more you will start to transform your day, your experience, as well as your entire life.

Final Thoughts...

Before we close, let's explore the question that we started this whole craziness with...

What is the true purpose of meditation? Is it to quiet the mind? Sure, it can be.

Is it to connect with your deeper self? Most definitely. That is a wonderful goal.

Is it to enjoy all the benefits that meditation will provide you? Why not! You'll be getting them anyway, so you might as well receive openly and happily.

Yes, all of that is great.

But, the true purpose of meditation is to simply **be**. Without any expectations or hopes about what you'll get or where you'll end up.

And, it is to realize that where it eventually takes you is not important. Also, how you get to wherever you go isn't really important either. And ultimately, how long it takes you to get there is also not that important.

It's what you're doing - or *not* doing, really - while you journey to that place, and even when you do reach that place...wherever that may be.

So, the true purpose of meditation is to simply *practice* it often. Practice sitting in stillness and just *being*.

And, heck, if any of the above reasons or benefits can help and motivate you into practicing everyday, then use them. Use whatever you need to make this a daily practice.

Whether you do the formal sit-down meditation, the waking 'present moment' meditation, or (hopefully) both, you should make it a point to practice meditating as often as possible.

If all you do right now is to promise yourself to meditate regularly for the next 30 days, I guarantee that you will start seeing some very cool shifts and improvements in your life, as well as in your mental and physical health.

I hope you will give yourself this gift. It costs you just a few minutes per day, and it pays you in really big ways... with a better, healthier, happier, and more peaceful life.

Respectfully Raise Your Vibration and Raise Your Life,

Daniel Amos

The author, publisher, and distributor of this product assume no responsibility for the use or misuse of this product, or for any injury, damage and/or financial loss sustained to persons or property as a result of using this report. The liability, negligence, use, misuse or abuse of the operation of any methods, strategies, instructions or ideas contained in the material herein is the sole responsibility of the reader.